Learning on the Go:

How to Personalize Education with the iPad

LUIS F.

CAST SKINNY BOOKS

UNTIL LEARNING HAS NO LIMITS™

Bulk discounts available: For details, email publishing@cast.org or visit www.castpublishing.org.

Library of Congress Control Number: 2018933982

Paperback ISBN 978-1-930583-24-5
Ebook ISBN 978-1-930583-25-2

Published by:
CAST Professional Publishing
an imprint of CAST, Inc.
Wakefield, Massachusetts, USA

Cover and interior design by Happenstance Type-O-Rama

Printed in the United States of America

Contents

About the Author

As someone with a visual impairment, Luis F. Pérez, PhD, knows firsthand how technology can improve the lives of people with disabilities in a meaningful way. He shares his personal experience and expertise in the field of inclusive design as a consultant, speaker, and author.

Dr. Pérez is a Technical Assistance Specialist at the National Center on Accessible Educational Materials (AEM Center) at CAST. He earned his doctorate in special education from the University of South Florida, and in 2009, he was named an Apple Distinguished Educator.

He is the author of *Mobile Learning for All: Supporting Accessibility with the iPad* from Corwin Press, and his work has appeared in numerous education and technology journals. *Learning on the Go* is his first book for CAST Professional Publishing.

Dr. Pérez is President-Elect of ISTE's Inclusive Learning Network, which previously selected him as its Outstanding Inclusive Educator in 2016.

To learn more about his resources for educators, including eBooks and video tutorials, visit his website or follow him on Twitter *@eyeonaxs*.

Introduction

"[A computer is] the most remarkable tool that we've ever come up with...it's the equivalent of a bicycle for our minds."
—STEVE JOBS

The late Steve Jobs understood that the power of technology lies in its ability to amplify human ability, not in the tool itself. Thus, he believed that just as a bicycle makes it easier for a rider to get from point A to point B, a computer could do the same thing for cognitive tasks such as learning.

When Jobs compared the computer to a "bicycle for the mind," the computer he was referring to typically sat on a desk and was fairly heavy and expensive. Today, the same computing power is available in one of the devices most of us carry in our pockets. In fact, even the most inexpensive smartphone or tablet is exponentially faster and more powerful than the computer that took us to the moon, one of our greatest technical achievements. A touchscreen device like the Apple iPad can be a word processor one minute and, with a few taps, stand in for a drum machine or a drawing canvas the next. And these devices are filled with accessibility features and customizable displays.

This flexibility makes the iPad an ideal tool for implementing Universal Design for Learning (UDL), an approach for designing a flexible curriculum that can accommodate the needs of an increasingly variable and diverse learner population. If you are new to UDL or just want to brush up on the principles and guidelines, check out *Universal Design for Learning: Theory & Practice* (Meyer, Rose, & Gordon, 2014), a free online book at udltheorypractice.cast.org (email registration required).

To be clear, UDL is not dependent on technology. Rather, it's a way to balance learning supports and challenges to meet the needs of highly variable learners. Creative educators who adopt the UDL mindset of flexibility and choice over one-size-fits-all solutions can and do implement UDL successfully even when there is little or no technology available.

But the flexibility that technology offers can make it easier for educators to provide the options some learners need to be successful. Furthermore, for some learners, there is no UDL without technology. These learners would simply not be able to access any of the choices offered to them within a UDL environment. Finally, building proficiency with technology, though it should not become the be-all and end-all of education, is an important goal by itself. To be future ready, learners need to develop the digital literacies that will allow them to thrive in a culture that is increasingly built around technology and media.

To return to the bicycle metaphor, when we learn to ride a bike, we begin with supports—training wheels, an adult who is there to cheer us on and catch us when we are about to fall, and maybe an expert model of how to pedal and balance. Over time, we become more confident and develop the skill needed to ride on our own. Gradually, the supports are withdrawn. We continue to practice, perhaps in the safety of our driveways and then later in more challenging terrain. Eventually, we become expert riders. A bicycle often has an adjustable seat so that it can accommodate riders of different sizes. Each rider can find the optimal riding position for maximizing pedaling power, properly seeing the road ahead, and balance.

Learning in the UDL way is similar. We start with supports—sometimes lots of them—and gradually become expert learners. Similarly, flexible technologies provide educators with the tools to place each learner in the optimal position for learning, whether it is by customizing the display to suit the learner's ability to see, or turning on supports such as text to speech that can reduce the effort involved in reading.

Luis's Story

I discovered inclusive technology at a key point in my life, when I needed it most. In my early thirties, I was diagnosed with a condition called retinitis pigmentosa (RP for short) that results in the gradual loss of peripheral and low-light vision. For many people, RP eventually leads to complete blindness. The diagnosis of a visual impairment forced me to make several significant changes. The ability to drive was first to go, because it was no longer safe for me to be on the road. Suddenly, I had to rethink everything, from how I was going to get to work the next day to what kind of future I would have.

To be proactive, I decided to go back to school to pursue a graduate degree in education. However, I found it extremely difficult to keep up with the work, especially all the reading, while relying on my quickly fading eyesight. I was just about ready to throw in the towel and give up any hope of completing my degree when something magical happened. I heard the VoiceOver screen reader (a program that comes on new Mac computers, iPhones, iPads, and iPod touches) for the first time. That moment—which I have called "a magical moment"—changed my life.

What I heard didn't just speak to my ears—it spoke to my heart. Beyond the high quality of the VoiceOver voice, it was the message I received that was more important: "It's going to be okay. There are some very smart people working on technology that will allow you to remain an independent, productive person." Without the hope technology brought into my life at that time, I'm not so sure I would have been able to overcome the many challenges I encountered as I pursued my graduate education.

Fortunately, as my vision got worse, the speech and other accessibility features of the Mac were brought to the iPhone and the iPad, and they have continued to improve and keep pace with my needs. These mobile devices have now become the primary way I use these accessibility features. At least one of these devices is always with me, and the powerful cameras have played a key role in allowing me to continue my hobby of photography. I can no longer use a traditional camera with my visual impairment, but the accessibility of the iPhone and iPad have turned them into "a second set of eyes" for me, another way that I am able to document my experience with vision loss and enjoy the beauty of the world around us. I also use photography to support my advocacy work. It helps me challenge any preconceived ideas people might have about the things people with visual impairments can do.

I hope the tools you master with the help of this book provide that same kind of "magical moment" for each of your learners, and propel them into a bright future where they can realize their full potential.

PAUSE AND THINK   Now that I've shared with you why I have written this book, pause and think about your own personal goal for reading this book. What is it that you want to get out of it? Using a note-taking or drawing app on your device, jot down one goal that you have. At the end of each chapter, take time to revisit that goal.

Getting the Most Out of This Book

As I have traveled around the country doing presentations on mobile learning, I have been struck by two observations.

First, there is a misconception that you must install a lot of apps to get the full benefit of the iPad. Many powerful features are already built into the device, and one of my goals with this book is to make you more aware of these features and show you how to use them to their fullest.

Second, it's easy to become overwhelmed by the many options available in the App Store. Thousands of educational apps are available, with more arriving each day. To help you narrow them down to a more manageable toolkit, I have done much of the work for you in vetting and testing the apps mentioned in this book. They are the go-to apps I have found useful for not only myself but the individual diverse learners I support.

All you need to get the most from this book is an iPad with the latest version of its iOS operating system and a basic understanding of how the device works (how to navigate the interface and how to install, launch, and close apps). Although I will mostly refer to the iPad, the accessibility features mentioned in this book work in a similar way across all iOS devices, such as the iPhone. As of this writing, the current version of the iPad's operating system is iOS 11. You can find out what version your iPad is running by going to Settings > General > About > Version.

If you need to update to the latest version of iOS, you can do so right from the device if you are connected to a Wi-Fi network. Just go to Settings > General > Software Update and follow the prompts to download and install the update. You will also need to have a valid App Store account to install some of the apps mentioned. Most of these apps are free or offer a free version. As with the accessibility features, most apps will work on both the iPad and the iPhone, though they may look a bit different on the iPhone because of the smaller screen.

I focus on the iPad because it is the most popular tablet in use by educators today and has the largest, most diverse app store, especially when it comes to apps designed for education. Because of the smooth way Apple delivers updates, iPads also provide the most predictable experience for discussing UDL implementation. If you have updated to the latest version of iOS on your iPad, we will all be on the same page as I discuss some of the built-in features later in the book.

A note for Chromebook users: I am aware that a lot of school districts are "going Google" with Chromebooks due to their lower initial cost and ease of administration. The framework presented in this book can be implemented with Chromebooks, but there are limitations because the accessibility features on Chromebooks are not as well developed. For example, although Chromebooks include a basic screen reader called ChromeVox, as of this writing switch access is not available on these devices. Where appropriate, a QR code will point you to Chrome alternatives for apps mentioned in the book.

 A CLOSER LOOK   Throughout the book, you will see Quick Response (QR) codes that allow you to access additional information about the topics and ideas discussed in each chapter. The ability to scan QR codes is built into the Camera app with iOS 11, or you can use a number of free QR scanning apps (my favorite is i-nigma from 3GVision). Go ahead and give it a try—if you are successful, the QR code should open up to the resources for this introduction on the book's companion website.

Key Takeaways

- As Steve Jobs noted, the importance of technology lies in what it allows us to accomplish and not in the tool itself.

- The high level of personalization that is possible with the iPad makes it an ideal tool for creating the "adjustable seats for learning" our diverse learners need to access the curriculum and develop their learning expertise.

- UDL is first and foremost about flexible pedagogy, but technology can make the implementation of UDL easier. Proficiency with technology is also in itself an important skill for learners to master if they are to be future ready.

1

The iPad, Mobile Learning, and UDL

Tools come and go, especially given the rapid pace of technological change. A framework can provide us with a shared vision and plan of practice by signaling the values we want to bring to our learning designs. In this book, we'll rely on the Universal Design for Learning (UDL) principles and guidelines to lead our use of technology supports. A key value we share when using UDL is to seek greater equity in education by allowing each person to tap into his or her full potential and expertise.

In the case of the iPad, three unique features make it an ideal tool for supporting the implementation of a flexible and inclusive pedagogy based on UDL: its portability; its robust, built-in accessibility; and its powerful media creation capabilities. Each of these unique features corresponds to one of the three UDL principles of multiple means of engagement, representation, and action and expression.

iPad as a Support for Multiple Means of Engagement

As educators, we know how important it is to build learning environments that favor authentic, engaging experiences, and research confirms this (Lave & Wenger, 1990). People learn best when the learning experience is meaningful and relevant to the individual—when the student can say, "I get the point of this." As Traxler (2007) explains, small and portable mobile devices can engage learners in active tasks such as data capture, location awareness, and collaborative work (through messaging apps) while they are still embedded in the environment where the task takes place. The difference between "book" learning and what's called *situated learning* is the difference between riding a stationary bike indoors and riding a "real" bike out on the road or trail to experience the great outdoors.

For example, situated learning can involve using the cameras and microphones built into mobile devices to document a real-world problem such as pollution and its impact on the community. Instead of merely reading or watching a program about this problem, learners can go out into their communities, participate in a clean-up project with a local agency, and document the problem through photos, videos, and interviews. The data learners collect can then be used to create a presentation that raises awareness about an aspect of pollution. This kind of situated learning is consistent with the UDL principle of multiple means of engagement (UDL: Recruit interest; Optimize relevance; value, and authenticity).

PAUSE AND THINK　Think back to some of the situated learning experiences you have had in your life, such as visiting a farm, engaging in community service, and the like. What are some of the things you could have done with a mobile device to make that learning experience more meaningful?

iPad as a Support for Multiple Means of Representation

Of course, an engaging experience also depends on an engaging and *appropriate* presentation of content. For students with disabilities, content that is not accessible is practically useless. Although technology integration should aim for more than just basic access to information, accessibility is foundational and nonnegotiable—just as it is in public buildings, transportation, parks, and other open environments.

Fortunately, the iPad includes several built-in accessibility features that allow it to provide many of the same supports as traditional assistive technologies but in a consumer device that does not have the same stigma and cost of more specialized solutions. The iPad's Voice-Over screen reader is one example of a built-in feature that improves access to information for learners with visual impairments. Similarly, features such as Zoom and Magnifier offer options for customizing the display of visual information and the built-in support for closed captions provides an alternative for auditory content (UDL: Provide options for perception). We explore the iPad's built-in accessibility features in more detail in chapter 2.

One of the key advantages of the iPad is that learners can now make some of the needed adjustments to the content on their own. In some ways, this means learners now "bring accessibility with them," but they may not always be aware that the features they need are already built into their devices. As an educator, you should make your learners aware of the great power their devices already hold that let them personalize their education. By removing barriers to learning and reducing the frustrations many learners experience, the iPad can also boost engagement.

In addition to its built-in accessibility features that are specifically designed to improve access to information for people with disabilities, the iPad includes several supports for reading that can help all learners overcome the limitations of print. Print still dominates much of the content used in education, but as a fixed format it can present challenges to learners who need adjustments such as larger text or text to speech to support decoding. The iPad's robust text-to-speech system has high-quality voices as well as options for customizing the display by adjusting the text size, enabling a high-contrast view, and more (UDL: Offer options for customizing the display of information; Support decoding text, mathematical notation, and symbols). We explore many of the supports for reading available on the iPad in more detail in chapter 3.

iPad as a Support for Multiple Means of Action and Expression

Engaging, effective learning environments also give students the means to carry out learning tasks and express themselves in authentic ways. New mobile technologies can play a big part in helping learners be active participants in their own education, with teachers facilitating rather than dictating the learning process. Learners create understanding rather than merely consume information, and their own voice and perspective become important to the learning process. A good example of this happens when students use mobile devices to collect data, record interviews, and share what they know in real-world, real-time settings.

In chapter 4, we will explore the many ways learners can use the iPad to demonstrate understanding using a variety of media (UDL: Vary the methods for response and navigation; Use multiple media for communication; Use multiple tools for construction and composition). We will also explore how to take advantage of the powerful cameras and the microphone built into the iPad to give learners a rich palette of choices for their creative expression. With these tools, we can allow the writer to write, the artist to paint or draw, and the photographer or budding filmmaker to show their learning using their preferred tools. These choices make learning more personalized for the talents and interests of each learner (UDL: Provide options for recruiting interest; Optimize individual choice and autonomy).

In chapter 5, we will explore several apps learners can use to publish their work to a wider audience. Knowing that their work will be shared more widely can often raise the bar for the effort and care learners put into their work, and the collaboration with a broader online community provides a more authentic experience that mirrors the future world of work learners will experience (UDL: Foster collaboration and community; Promote expectations and beliefs that optimize motivation).

 A CLOSER LOOK   Scan the QR code to access additional resources for this chapter on the companion website.

Key Takeaways

- The UDL framework provides us with a common vision and a practical approach to helping each person tap his or her full creative potential and expertise.

- The portability of the iPad makes it an ideal tool for situating learning beyond the four walls of the classroom to make it more authentic and engaging.

- The built-in accessibility features of the iPad allow learners to "bring accessibility with them" to customize the learning environment and benefit from multiple means of representation.

- The iPad's powerful cameras and microphone, along with a rich collection of content creation apps, provide a rich palette for learners to creatively express their understanding and develop a strong personal voice.

2

Access to Content and Tools

MEDIA INTRODUCTION

Scan the QR code to hear an audio introduction for this chapter as voiced by the VoiceOver screen reader on the iPad.

How would you ride a bicycle if you couldn't see where you were going? The short answer is that you wouldn't, at least not independently.

I would know, because prior to being diagnosed with a visual impairment I enjoyed riding a bicycle for exercise. After my diagnosis, my only option was to rent or buy a tandem bike (which is much more expensive and harder to locate than a regular one), and then find someone who would be a good riding partner—someone with a compatible riding profile and schedule.

Fortunately, I did not have the same limitations as a graduate student when it came to the technology and learning materials I needed. The mobile devices I used had adjustable settings so I could read the text without a great deal of effort, and I could turn on the text-to-speech feature for those times when my eyes were just too tired to read. More important, the availability of these accessibility features gave me hope that even if I lost my eyesight completely, the technology could help me work around these challenges. This kept me from getting discouraged during the tough times of my journey with vision loss.

In this chapter, I examine several of the iPad's built-in accessibility features. These features help remove barriers in the learning environment to ensure that all learners can interact with their touchscreen devices, enjoy equal access to information, and independently communicate their basic needs to those around them.

The features in this chapter are specifically designed for people with disabilities. The "universal" part of UDL means we have to address the entire spectrum of human ability, including the needs of learners who have disabilities.

However, this chapter is important for general educators, too. With inclusion initiatives gaining momentum, you never know when one of these learners is going to end up in your classroom. You don't need to be an expert with VoiceOver, Switch Control, and the other features discussed in this chapter, but just knowing these features exist and having a basic understanding of how they work will at a minimum make it easier for you to collaborate with teachers of the visually impaired (TVIs), speech language pathologists (SLPs), and other professionals who support you and your learners.

Access to the Interface

One of the challenges of using a touchscreen is that not everyone has the fine motor skills to perform the precise taps and other gestures required for navigation, interaction, and response. Before learners can make use of the information presented on an iPad, they must be able to navigate the interface and open the apps or websites where this information is available. Built-in iPad accessibility features such as Touch Accommodations, AssistiveTouch, and Switch Control can facilitate access to the touchscreen for those with motor difficulties.

 SMART TIP With the Siri personal assistant built into iOS, learners can send a text message, check for new email, and much more, often without typing a single word or even needing to touch the screen. To learn about all things Siri can do, just say, "What can you do?" once you activate the personal assistant.

Touch Accommodations

Touch Accommodations can be helpful for those who have tremors that result in unwanted taps. You can specify a Hold Duration setting so that a hold is required before a button is activated. With Tap Assistance, you don't have to be as precise with where you tap the screen to perform a selection. You can choose to have the iPad recognize either your initial or your final touch location.

AssistiveTouch

The few physical buttons needed to operate an iPad can pose a challenge for some learners. AssistiveTouch provides on-screen alternatives for these physical buttons, including the Home button and the volume buttons on the side of the device. In fact, I know a lot of people who use AssistiveTouch because the Home button on their devices is no longer functional. AssistiveTouch also allows learners with motor challenges to perform multitouch gestures (those that involve more than one finger) with a single tap. In some cases, this may be done with a mouth stick or a head-mounted pointer if the learner cannot hold a stylus to perform the tap. AssistiveTouch even has an option for saving more complex multitouch gestures so they can be accessed and performed from an on-screen menu with a series of taps.

 SMART TIP   The AssistiveTouch icon makes for a nice pointer when demonstrating how to use the iPad. I frequently use this option to direct attention when mirroring my iPad's screen to a projector.

Switch Control

With Switch Control, learners who have significant motor challenges can interact with any part of the iOS interface of the iPad through a two-step process. First, the learner will wait for a cursor to sequentially scan through the various options shown on the screen; then when the cursor gets to the option the learner wants, he or she will tap the screen, press an external button, or perform a left- or right-head movement (though this last option is not as reliable as of this writing). For those who are not ready for the timing demands of automatic scanning, there is also the option to use two switches: one switch will move the cursor, and the other selects an action. When this selection is made, a menu will pop up with actions ranging from a simple tap to complex multitouch gestures such as swipes. Learners who have conditions such as cerebral palsy that make muscle control difficult can still use the iPad with the help of Switch Control.

Since Switch Control is intended for people who would otherwise not be able to use a touchscreen, it changes how you interact with your iPad. When Switch Control is turned on, you are not able to just tap a button to turn it off. For this reason, you should set up the Accessibility Shortcut to allow you to quickly turn Switch Control off with a triple-click of your iPad's Home button. You can do this by going to Settings > General > Accessibility > Accessibility Shortcut and making sure Switch Control is the only option with a checkmark next to its name (this may require you to temporarily turn off other features that also use a triple-click of the Home button, such as Magnifier or Guided Access). The Accessibility Shortcut will give you a way to safely explore the use of Switch Control.

Access to Information

The iPad and other iOS devices include several built-in features for providing multiple means of representation to account for the variability with which learners perceive information. These include Zoom and Magnifier (UDL: Offer ways of customizing the display of information), audio descriptions and closed captions (UDL: Offer alternatives for visual/auditory information), and Voice-Over (UDL: Offer alternatives for visual information).

Zoom

Zoom is the built-in screen magnification feature on the iPad. Originally, Zoom worked only in a full-screen mode. However, since the release of iOS 8, Zoom also supports a window mode. In this mode, a small window magnifies only a specific area of the screen while the area outside the window remains at 100 percent magnification. In addition, Zoom also supports a variety of lenses for adjusting the appearance of the zoomed-in area of the screen. Like several iOS accessibility features, Zoom is gestured based: a three-finger double-tap is used to zoom in and out, and dragging with three fingers while zoomed in changes what is shown on the screen.

In addition to helping learners with low vision, Zoom can be a useful teaching aid. By "zooming" in, teachers can highlight the key information (UDL: Highlight critical features). Zoom can also be used for hide-and-reveal activities where only the prompt is visible at a high magnification level. After giving learners time to reflect on the prompt, teachers can slide the answer into view to complete the activity (UDL: Guide information processing).

Magnifier

Sometimes we need to magnify objects in the environment. For example, connecting small circuits in a science project may be difficult for any learner due to the size of the circuits but will present an even bigger challenge to someone with low vision. Magnifier (iOS 10 and above) can help in this kind of situation. Activated with a triple-click of the Home button, Magnifier leverages the full resolution of the cameras on the iPad to provide a clear picture. In addition to being able to freeze the image for closer inspection, learners can apply a number of color filters and adjust the brightness and contrast (UDL: Customize the display of information).

Audio Description and Closed Captions

Audio descriptions allow someone who is unable to see to instead hear a description of the action taking place in a video. These descriptions are provided as a secondary audio track that can be turned on in your iPad's accessibility settings.

Closed captions are the strip of text displayed at the bottom of the screen as an alternative representation of the audio content in a video program (UDL: Offer alternatives for auditory information). They are one of the best examples of universal design, because they were originally developed in the 1970s for the benefit of people who are deaf or hard of hearing but now have many uses in a variety of situations. For example, you may see them turned on at the gym, at a restaurant, at the airport, or anywhere the audio is difficult to hear. In the classroom, captioning can help if the speakers do not work, or if the audio is of poor quality or the speaker has a strong accent.

Beyond these accessibility considerations, captions (or same-language subtitles, as they are sometimes called in the literature) are helpful for children and adults learning to read (Gemsbacher, 2015). If a video includes closed captions, they can be shown by default by enabling them in Settings on your iOS device. You can even customize the appearance of these captions by making the text larger, changing the font, and adding a drop shadow or outline to make them stand out from the video so that they are easier to read.

VoiceOver

A screen reader is software that allows people who are blind to listen to content they would otherwise not be able to see on a display (UDL: Offer alternatives for visual information). On the iPad, the screen reader VoiceOver is included as a standard feature that is available out of the box, without the need to install a separate app. Voice-Over is a gesture-based screen reader that is designed for touchscreens. As the user moves a finger around on the screen, VoiceOver reads the content that is underneath—whether it is some text, an app, or a button or other interface element.

Starting with iOS 8, VoiceOver can do this with a high-quality voice called Alex. This voice must be downloaded the first time you want to use it, but it is then available even when you are not connected to the Internet. Alex does some text processing in the background for improved pronunciation of difficult words; for those times when it doesn't work as well, such as with some proper names, a pronunciation editor is available as of iOS 10. Voice-Over also supports output to a separate Braille display for someone who reads in that format (this is also helpful for individuals who are both blind and deaf). An extensive set of other gestures allows the user to navigate through the options on the screen in a variety of ways, adjust the speaking rate, and much more. A built-in help feature for practicing these gestures makes it easy to develop proficiency with the screen reader, and the VO Starter app provides an interactive tutorial for even more practice.

SMART TIP   Use Siri to quickly "turn VoiceOver on/off." Siri works for a few other accessibility features you can activate with your voice, such as Invert Colors and Speak Screen.

Access to Communication

The iPad can be a cost-effective alternative to the dedicated speech-generating devices many learners have used in the past. Although alternative and augmentative communication (AAC) apps are among the most expensive in the App Store, the combined cost of an iPad with a sophisticated AAC app is still lower than that of a dedicated speech-generating device. An in-depth discussion of AAC apps and language acquisition is best done in consultation with a trained speech language professional who is familiar with best practices in that field. However, you should at least have a basic understanding of the most common types of apps that are available for speech support on the iPad.

Most AAC apps fall into one of two categories: *symbol-based* or *text-based*. Symbol-based apps such as Proloquo2Go are intended for learners who are developing literacy. The learner is presented with a grid of symbols or pictures, each of which represents a word or expression. The learner can combine them into full phrases that can be spoken aloud with a synthesized voice. The pictures or symbols are not placed in a random order on the screen; a great deal of research has gone into figuring out the optimal arrangement to facilitate efficient communication.

At a minimum, the AAC app you choose should support what is known as a "core vocabulary," a system that emphasizes the core words that are most frequently used in conversation (they make up about 80 percent or more of what we say). Other words, considered fringe vocabulary, are placed less prominently but are still available to the learner as needed.

Text-based AAC apps help those who have developed literacy and just need the device to produce speech with a synthesized voice. An example of this type of app is Proloquo4Text, from the same company that makes Proloquo2Go (AssistiveWare). With this app, learners can either rely on preset phrases or build their own so that they can be easily accessed and spoken aloud when greeting strangers on the street, ordering lunch at a restaurant, and more.

GOING GOOGLE

Chromebooks boast several accessibility features, including screen magnification and the ChromeVox screen reader. However, they lack a robust switch access solution. Scan the QR code to learn more about the Chromebook accessibility features that correspond to the iOS features discussed in this chapter.

Though not as robust as the other apps I have mentioned, the SoundingBoard app from AbleNet is free and can be useful in a pinch. As the name implies, the app is designed for creating communication boards that allow a learner to produce simple responses (such as Yes/No) or express basic needs. Each board can include up to 20 messages consisting of a symbol or an image taken with the iPad's camera, along with a message recorded with the device's microphone. A few premade boards are already included when the app is installed, and you can buy more from AbleNet if you do not feel like creating your own. Boards can have audio prompts for learners with visual impairments, and SoundingBoard also has built-in switch access support that works well when paired with AbleNet's switch interfaces (such as the Blue2).

 ## SKINNY SKETCH:
Logan Prickett

Growing up on a farm in Alabama, Logan Prickett was an active child who enjoyed several outdoor activities. At age 13, he had an allergic reaction to the contrast dye used during an MRI. His heart stopped beating for 45 minutes, and his time with limited oxygen left Logan blind, a wheelchair user, with fine motor difficulties, and unable to speak above a whisper due to damage to his vocal cords that occurred during life-saving measures. When Logan awoke after being in a coma for 12 days, he had to undergo extensive rounds of physical therapy. Remarkably for someone who had gone through such a traumatic event, Logan's cognitive abilities remained largely untouched. He soon found new ways to enjoy doing what he loves, including skiing, horseback riding, and even skydiving. Fully cognitively capable and gifted, Logan went on to graduate from high school and enrolled at Auburn University at Montgomery (AUM), where he met his next big challenge: college algebra.

(continues)

(continued)

Learners who are blind can use Nemeth Braille to access math notation, but Logan is unable to feel the raised Braille dots due to some of his motor challenges. When Logan enrolled in his Intermediate Algebra class in the spring of 2015, he became the inspiration for the Logan Project at AUM. A key goal of this project is the development of a process-driven math (PDM) methodology that will allow learners like Logan to fully drive the intellectual processes involved in simplifying and solving algebraic expressions and equations, all while using only audio.

I first met Logan when his family and support team from the Logan Project visited with me following a presentation I did at a rehabilitation facility in Tennessee. At that time, we set a simple goal for Logan: to get started on the journey to independent communication, beginning with the ability to send and receive short messages with his family and those close to him. Using a combination of the built-in iOS Switch Control and an app called Workflow, we soon had Logan independently sending emails, text messages, and more. This was important for giving Logan back a sense of independence. As he has stated,

> *It really helps. Now I don't have to ask my mom to check it so it helps other people, too. I heard the other day on my email that there was going to be a quiz in biology that I had not known about, so it is giving me more independence in my schoolwork. I like the fact that I know what is happening and I can do something about it.*

Over time, the communication system has evolved to incorporate some alternative and augmentative communication (AAC). For example, Logan used an AAC voice

(continues)

(continued)

with a Southern accent to present with the rest of the Logan Project team at the 2017 California State University, Northridge, assistive technology conference in San Diego. We are even using an Amazon Echo smart speaker to allow Logan to access his favorite news sources, including podcasts, the local weather, and research articles for school that can be read aloud by the Echo's synthesized speech. After successfully completing his math requirements, Logan is now pursuing a degree in psychology at AUM. He is also employed by the Logan Project, providing expert advice to the development of PDM. Finally, Logan has accomplished a rare feat for an undergraduate student: he is listed as a co-author on a book chapter and a journal article. His future is bright.

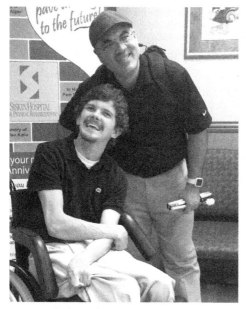

Logan with the author. PHOTO: ANN GULLEY

A CLOSER LOOK   Scan the QR code to access additional resources for this chapter on the companion website, including student activities and closed-captioned videos that show the accessibility features in action.

 Key Takeaways

- The iPad's built-in accessibility features make the touchscreen interface accessible, lowering barriers to learning.

- Learners with low vision can use tools like Zoom, Magnifier, and VoiceOver with their iOS devices to get the same assistance that used to require dedicated devices.

- AssistiveTouch and Switch Control are two features of iOS that make the interface more accessible to individuals who have motor difficulties.

- The iPad is a cost-effective alternative to traditional speech-generating devices. It supports several communication apps for learners who have speech difficulties.

3

Built-In Supports and Scaffolds for Variability

MEDIA INTRODUCTION

Scan the QR code to watch a brief video introduction for this chapter.

The technologies we explored in the previous chapter harken back to the origins of UDL as an attempt to address the needs of "learners in the margins." By addressing the needs of marginalized learners, we find solutions that benefit everyone. In short, by using the UDL framework, we recognize that all learners are on a continuum of ability and disability, and that the natural variability of individuals means that one-size-fits-all solutions seldom work for anyone. Throughout this chapter, you will see many examples of this philosophy in action as we look at apps and built-in iPad features that can benefit all learners, not just those who have been identified with learning difficulties.

PAUSE AND THINK   Can you think of some ways in which you exhibit variability? Are you more successful when you read in long sessions or divide up the reading with short breaks in between? Does it help to first look at the digital resources before you read the rest of the content, or vice versa? In what other ways do you vary as a reader?

GET THE APPS

This chapter mentions quite a few apps. Scan the QR code to see a full list of the apps in the order they are mentioned.

Display Accommodations

Sometimes, removing a barrier to learning can be as simple as adjusting the text size so that the reader doesn't have to spend as much effort trying to read text that is too small. On the iPad, the text size and other display options can be easily adjusted in the Vision section of the Accessibility settings (UDL: Offer ways of customizing the display of information). Most of these options involve simple toggles. This means you can safely try different settings until you find the ones that work just for you. You can always tap the same buttons to undo your changes.

One of my favorite display accommodations on the iPad is Invert Colors. It reverses the colors so that there is a dark background with light text (the default is dark text on a light background). In addition to being essential for those of us who have low vision and need higher contrast, this option can be helpful when reading on a touch-screen outdoors or in bright lighting. Starting with iOS 11, Invert Colors has a Smart Invert option that leaves media such as photos and videos alone when Invert Colors is activated. This can be helpful when the photo or video has important information that would be difficult to read when the colors are inverted.

In addition to the display accommodations that are part of iOS, iBooks and other e-book reading apps will often include their own options for adjusting the text size, changing the font, and turning on a night mode for better contrast. The Safari web browser on iOS devices has a similar feature called Reader. This is a special view where only the text and a few images are shown to the reader—the ads, navigation, and other distracting content are hidden out of view to improve focus. Once the Reader view has been enabled, you can adjust the text size, change the font, and switch to a high-contrast view just as you can when reading in iBooks.

Text to Speech

Text to speech can be a valuable support for different learners. I often use the built-in text to speech when my eyes get tired so that I can save myself from eye-strain. Other learners use it as a support for decoding, an area where dyslexics and those with other learning difficulties tend to struggle. The Speech pane found under Vision organizes settings for the iOS text-to-speech features in one place. The two main ones are Speak Selection and Speak Screen. The only difference between the two is in how you activate the text to speech. With Speak Selection you must select some text first, and then choose the Speak option from a menu to hear the selected text read aloud. Speak Screen does not require you to do this. Instead, you perform a special gesture (swiping down with two fingers from the top of the screen) and the device will speak everything that is on the display (including the buttons and other interface elements). If you activate the feature while reading an e-book or other multipage document, it will continuously read and even automatically flip the pages.

 SMART TIP   Use Siri to activate Speak Screen if you can't perform the special gesture. Just say "speak screen," and you should hear the items on the screen read aloud.

Both Speak Selection and Speak Screen support word and sentence highlighting, as well as text/background color combinations, as content is read aloud, which can help focus attention while reading. You can even choose from two different styles for the sentence highlighting, and the voice used by the text to speech is also customizable. Both iOS features can also use the same high-quality Alex voice that is available for the VoiceOver screen reader. Learners who speak languages other than English can choose from several languages for the iOS text to speech, and for some languages they can even choose different dialects (such as Spanish from Spain or Mexico). Many of the dialects allow you to download enhanced-quality voices for even better results, but note that like Alex these voices take up some space on your device.

As good as the built-in iOS text-to-speech feature is, sometimes you may need more customization than it offers. Voice Dream Reader provides more choices for word color and sentence highlighting as well as text/background combinations. Other features include masking to reveal only a few lines of text at a time, and a Pac-man mode that removes the words as they are read to limit distractions. Voice Dream Reader also includes a couple of dyslexia-friendly fonts: OpenDyslexic and Dyslexie. Voice Dream Reader is also a good way to access books from the Bookshare service, a free source of learning materials for school-age learners who have qualifying disabilities (a subscription option is also available). The flexibility of the Voice Dream Reader app makes it a nice complement to the built-in text to speech of iOS.

GOING GOOGLE

Scan the QR code to learn about reading, math, and executive functioning supports that are available for Google Chrome and Chromebooks.

Sometimes it is necessary to convert content that is in a print format into digital text before learners can use text to speech. Fortunately, several mobile apps are now available that can take a picture of the print material and perform optical character recognition (OCR). This is the process by which the individual characters on a printed page are scanned and converted into editable and searchable digital text. Two of my favorite apps for this kind of scanning are kNFB Reader and Prizmo (which has a Prizmo Go version meant for quick scans).

Some learners may need to have content translated into their native languages to help with understanding while they build proficiency in the target language. Two of my favorite apps for translation on the iPad are Google Translate and Microsoft Translator (UDL: Promote understanding across languages). Translations can be performed in different ways: by typing, speaking into the device, taking a photo, or even through handwriting.

 SMART TIP   Starting with iOS 11, Siri can perform quick translations. Just ask, "How do you say" followed by the word or phrase you want translated and the language (i.e., "How do you say where is the bathroom in Spanish?").

Despite the advances in text-to-speech quality, some learners may still prefer to listen to a recording of a human voice. Human narration can capture some of the inflection and tone that is sometimes lost with even the best text to speech. For learners who prefer audiobooks, the Learning Ally Link iPad app can be used to download narrated books from the Learning Ally subscription service. The Audible app also provides access to popular titles, sometimes read by the author him- or herself.

Supports for Math

Just as some learners struggle to decode print, others struggle with mathematical notation and symbols. These struggles can have an impact on their motivation to learn math, and they can get in the way of developing the basic math skills learners can build on for success with this subject later in life. My experience is illustrative. As an English language learner, I spent most of my first year in the United States (sixth grade) learning a new language, and I missed out on much of the math instruction. Falling behind impacted not only my motivation to learn math, but also nearly cost me a scholarship when I got to high school and struggled to meet a basic math requirement for admission to my prep school. I can only wonder how much better my experience with math would have been with some of the tools available today.

On the iPad, the built-in Calculator app fully supports VoiceOver for learners who are blind. For other learners, third-party calculator apps such as Talking Calculator and MyScript Calculator provide high-contrast modes, text to speech, and motor supports. Other math apps can be used for extra practice so that learners develop automaticity with skills ranging from basic number concepts to algebraic relationships. The portability of the iPad and other mobile devices means practice can take place anywhere the device can go. Some helpful math apps for iOS devices include Base Ten Math (virtual manipulatives, place value), the Math Learning Center Apps (fractions, place value, currency), and Algebra Touch (basic algebra concepts).

Sometimes a short video tutorial can be helpful for reviewing a challenging math concept. Khan Academy features a site that already includes many of these tutorials on a range of math-related topics. These videos are captioned and include interactive transcripts for accessibility. As great as Khan Academy is, sometimes it is helpful to create a more targeted tutorial with a whiteboard app to address a specific need. This can be quickly done with whiteboard apps such as Explain Everything. With it, you can record your voice as you explain concepts on the whiteboard, and then post the resulting video for your learners to download and watch when convenient.

 SMART TIP   With OS 11, you can do narrated screen recordings that are not limited to a specific app. For more details, visit the companion website, which you can access by scanning the QR code at the end of the chapter.

Supports for Executive Functioning

Executive functioning refers to the set of skills learners need to master to act strategically in pursuit of a goal. These include the ability to set priorities, develop a plan, and stay on task to see that plan through to completion. Expert learners have well-developed executive functioning that allows them to perform these skills with minimal prompting, whereas novices may need some of the supports mentioned in this section.

Guided Access

This feature has been marketed as a way for parents and caregivers to control or limit screen time, but I think learners themselves can use it to create a distraction-free work environment (UDL: Minimize threats and distractions). Once Guided Access has been enabled in Settings, a triple-click of the Home button will lock the iPad into the current app. At that point, the only way to exit to the Home screen is to once again triple-click the Home button and enter a passcode. There is also the option to set a timer that will lock the device when time expires.

In addition to locking the device into a single app, Guided Access can be used to disable parts of the screen. For example, you may not want a learner to access the settings area of an app once you have customized it. You can disable the part of the screen that corresponds to the settings button by drawing over it while the Guided Access options screen is visible.

 SMART TIP   As helpful as notifications can be for letting you know what needs to be done, sometimes they can be distracting. Go into Settings and disable the ones you don't need in Notifications.

Visual Schedules

Visual schedules tell a learner who struggles with transitions what activities will take place and in what order. To accommodate young learners, or those who have limited literacy, the schedules incorporate visuals in the form of symbols or images to represent each step of a routine. Just knowing what is expected can reduce the anxiety level for some learners. Visual schedules are also helpful for task analysis, where a complex task can be broken down into smaller steps that are more manageable for the learner (UDL: Guide information processing, visualization, and manipulation). Some of my favorite apps for creating visual schedules are Choiceworks, First Then Visual Schedule (FTVS HD), and CanPlan.

One thing to look for with visual schedule apps is that they allow you to include photos and videos taken with the iPad's camera as well as audio prompts recorded with the device's microphone. This is important for matching the schedules to the environment where the learner will be expected to perform the activities or behaviors (UDL: Optimize relevance, value, and authenticity).

 SMART TIP   Any app that allows you to lay out a series of photos in the desired sequence can be used to build a visual schedule. I often use the Book Creator app.

Time Management

For learners who struggle with time management, iOS includes the built-in apps Calendars, Reminders, and Clock. Each of these apps supports alarms or alerts that can remind a learner when important tasks are due. On the iPhone, which has GPS capabilities, tasks can even be set up to alert the learner when he or she arrives at or leaves a specific location (i.e., pick up my textbook before leaving the house).

SMART TIP   For time management apps, I recommend you choose the Alert option for its notification. With a banner, the alert goes away on its own after a short delay, and it can be easy to miss it.

As with other categories, there is an extensive selection of time management apps in the App Store. I personally use Fantastical 2 to help me manage my calendar and reminders. I also use timer apps while I work, including 30/30, Time Timer, and TimeWinder. I especially like TimeWinder because it has built-in support for the Pomodoro Technique. The Pomodoro Technique is a productivity method that involves intervals of 25-minute work periods followed by 5-minute breaks. I am using the Pomodoro Technique to help me write this book.

Note-taking and Information Management

Several note-taking apps can help learners keep important information close at hand and ensure it is not lost by backing it up to the cloud (UDL: Facilitate managing information and resources). The built-in Notes app is a good basic note-taking app. It backs up and syncs the notes across your Apple devices using the iCloud service. With a recent update, you can add basic drawings to your notes, as well as attach images taken with your device. Another great addition is the option to create a quick checklist by selecting some text and tapping the checklist button on the keyboard. A new item will then be created each time you press Return. Learners can use this feature to create quick checklists of the tasks or steps needed to complete a project (UDL: Enhance capacity for monitoring progress).

Text is not the only way you can take notes. Snapping a photo is often a quicker way to capture what appears on a whiteboard or on a presentation. Some apps also allow you to record audio along with your notes, and drawing or sketchnoting has become a popular way to visually capture information during live events. Some popular note-taking apps include Just Press Record (audio), Google Keep (multiple formats), Notability (multiple formats), and Paper by 53 (sketchnoting).

 SMART TIP   The updated Notes app in iOS 11 includes a document scanner for digitizing content from handouts and other print materials. You can then use the Markup feature to add highlighting and other annotations. This feature works very well with a good stylus like the Apple Pencil.

Situated Supports with QR Codes and AR

You have already experienced QR codes and seen how they can be used to link to additional online resources. These online resources can represent either background knowledge or additional content provided for enrichment. Augmented reality (AR) works in a similar way, but you don't have to scan a code for the online content to appear on your mobile device. AR has two "layers": the image, object, or place that acts as a trigger when scanned by a device with the appropriate app, and the digital content that is superimposed over the existing reality on the device's screen (the overlay). Once triggered, the digital content becomes visible to create a dynamic and often interactive experience for the viewer.

Both QR codes and AR can be used to provide just-in-time supports embedded in the environment. An example is a video with information on how to use a tool, or one that reminds learners of a strategy they can apply while reading a difficult text. The video would be accessed only if the learner needs the additional support and scans the QR code or holds the AR app over the area where the support is embedded. The free HP Reveal app can be used to both view and create simple AR experiences.

 ## SKINNY SKETCH: Curtis Coleman

As of this writing, Curtis has just recently completed eighth grade at a new school in Ontario, Canada. Eighth grade was a challenging year for Curtis, who has autism and often struggles with anxiety issues. He was given an iPad for learning support, but he had just started to explore some of the built-in accessibility features of the device when we spoke. For example, he sometimes uses the built-in text to speech to proofread what he has written.

For Curtis, it was a simple feature of the iPad we often take for granted that has made the biggest difference. As his mother explained when we spoke over video chat, Curtis loves to take photos. He is now learning to use this skill as an alternative way to take notes and save important information, including handouts and homework assignments.

(continues)

(continued)

This addresses Curtis's challenge with executive functioning—his tendency to misplace or lose important information he needs to complete his schoolwork. It has also reduced the anxiety he often feels when he must ask for handouts, since now he can capture the information himself. Having a photo of the information the teacher has shared is also helpful to Curtis's mom, who now has a better idea of what she needs to do at home to support Curtis with his schoolwork.

As Curtis's experience shows, sometimes we don't need an expensive app to make a difference in a learner's life. Sometimes, just leveraging the microphone and camera of the iPad can provide a powerful solution to a learning challenge. We will explore the multimedia capabilities of the iPad in more detail in the next chapter.

Curtis Coleman PHOTO: MARY ANN COLEMAN

A CLOSER LOOK Scan the QR code to access additional resources for this chapter, including student activities, on the companion website.

 # Key Takeaways

- Digital content is flexible and easy to personalize to the needs of diverse learners.

- The iPad includes a powerful text-to-speech engine that can support learners who struggle with decoding print. Apps such as Voice Dream Reader offer even more options for customization.

- Mathematical notation can be as problematic as print. Fortunately, several apps allow learners to practice basic math skills and build the automaticity needed for higher order math.

- The iPad can be an effective tool for learners who need help with executive functioning.

- QR codes and augmented reality (AR) can be used to provide situated supports available to learners in the environment at the time of need.

4

Leveraging Multimedia

MEDIA INTRODUCTION

Scan the QR code to watch a brief video introduction for this chapter.

The true power of the iPad lies in its flexibility. It's a word processor one minute, and with a few taps it becomes a drum machine or a drawing canvas the next. This makes the iPad a great fit for providing multiple means of action and expression, a key principle of UDL. Learners are no longer limited to text as the only means for showing their understanding and expressing their creativity. Learners can now demonstrate their learning by taking photos or recording videos that can be easily shared with not only their teachers and peers but also their parents and the rest of the community.

One way we can amplify our learners' voices with media is through a technique called "app smashing." App smashing is the process of taking the work created in one app, exporting it to a temporary location (typically the Camera Roll or an online service), and reimporting it into a second app, where it may be enhanced by adding overlays, recording narration, and more. The idea is that the sum (the final product) will be stronger than the parts (the items created by each app). The key to app smashing is making sure the apps you use can import and export content through the Camera Roll or an online service.

In this chapter, we will explore how learners can use the media creation features of the iPad not just to demonstrate their understanding in a variety of ways but also to start developing a powerful personal voice, one that is amplified by media. As you consider the apps in this chapter, ask yourself, "How can I enhance the content in this app with another app I know?"

GET THE APPS

This chapter mentions quite a few apps. Scan the QR code to see a full list of the apps in the order they are mentioned.

Supports for Writing

Although learners have several multimedia options to express themselves, sometimes writing is either the method they prefer or the one that works best for them. Thus, even with the range of new options we have at our disposal, we should not ignore writing as a means of expression. Sometimes, writing is itself the goal of a lesson. In that case, several supports are available as built-in options on the iPad to help us scaffold writing as needed.

Speech to Text and Word Prediction

For those who struggle with typing, the Dictation feature built into the on-screen keyboard can help. It allows you to use your voice to enter text (UDL: Vary the methods for response and navigation). To use Dictation, tap the microphone icon next to the spacebar on the on-screen keyboard, and then use your "radio announcer" voice to enunciate clearly as you speak your text into your device's microphone. If you do not see the microphone icon, make sure Enable Dictation is selected in Settings (General > Keyboards). For improved results, I recommend using the microphone on some headphones (like the ones that ship with the iPhone). As you speak the text, you can also dictate punctuation ("comma," "period") and use a few commands ("new paragraph," "all caps"). One thing to know is that Dictation may require you to be connected to the Internet for it to work on some devices that do not support an offline mode for this feature.

The word prediction feature built into iOS can also help with typing. As you type, suggestions appear on a strip above the on-screen keyboard. You can save time and effort by entering just the first few letters of a word and tapping the desired suggestion to add it to your text. If you don't see the word prediction suggestions, make sure Predictive is selected in Settings (this option is found under General > Keyboards). For longer phrases you type on a regular basis, you can set up shortcuts that expand into a full phrase when you press the spacebar. To set up these shortcuts, go to Settings > General > Keyboards and choose Text Replacement.

Third-Party Keyboards

Starting with iOS 8, it is possible to swap the built-in on-screen keyboard with several third-party options. These third-party keyboards can be customized in ways that are not possible with the built-in iOS on-screen keyboard. For example, you can select different themes that adjust the keyboard's appearance by changing the color of the keys, making them larger, and more. Third-party keyboards also tend to have better word prediction than the built-in iOS keyboard. These keyboards are installed from the App Store just like any other app. The third-party keyboard's app is where you customize the appearance and behavior of the keyboard. Once you have installed a third-party keyboard, you must go into Settings and tell iOS that you want to use your new third-party keyboard (by choosing General > Keyboard > Keyboards). Some third-party keyboards for iOS include Keeble, SuperKeys, Read&Write for iPad, and PhraseBoard.

Typing Feedback

Typing feedback was introduced in iOS 10 to help learners who tend to confuse letters as they write. The feature, which is found in the Speech section of the Accessibility settings, can provide feedback after each character or after each word. For the character feedback, you must wait a few seconds after typing the character to hear the built-in text to speech repeat it. You can determine the length of the delay in Settings (under General > Accessibility > Speech > Typing Feedback). With word feedback, you just press the spacebar to indicate a complete word. There is also an option (Hold to Speak Predictions) that will read the word prediction suggestions aloud as you move your finger over them. When you hear the desired word or phrase, all you do is lift your finger to enter it in your text.

Spell Check, Dictionary, and Grammar Support

Spell checking with automatic corrections (find this option in Settings > Keyboard) and a built-in dictionary help learners avoid common mistakes. To look up a word, double-tap it and choose Look Up from the popover menu. In Settings, you can choose from several dictionaries, including some in foreign languages. For additional dictionary support, you can download the free (ad-supported) Dictionary app. This app adds pronunciations for many words, a thesaurus, and a fun "word of the day" feature.

The Ginger Page app not only includes a dictionary and thesaurus, but also checks grammar and provides suggestions for different ways of rephrasing a sentence. It also includes a basic text-to-speech feature for proofreading.

Concept Mapping

Sometimes getting started with a writing assignment can be the hardest part. Concept mapping allows learners to start with a diagram of the key ideas or relationships and fill in the details later (UDL: Highlight patterns, critical features, big ideas, and relationships). Concept maps help learners keep their thoughts organized as they develop the structure for an essay or any other long writing project. They are also a great way for learners to capture and regularly review their goals in a more visual way (UDL: Guide appropriate goal setting; Heighten the salience of goals and objectives). Some concept mapping apps for iOS devices are Popplet, Inspiration Maps, and MindNode.

Word Processing

The App Store features an extensive selection of word processing apps. The ones I am highlighting here either do a good job of supporting the VoiceOver screen reader for accessibility or include other built-in learning supports such as word banks for vocabulary development. Word processing apps for iOS devices include Clicker Docs, Voice Dream Writer, iA Writer, and Pages.

GOING GOOGLE

Scan the QR code to learn about writing supports available for Google Chrome and Chromebooks.

SKINNY SKETCH:
Kaitlin

Kaitlin was a learner at the Fletcher School in Charlotte, North Carolina. The Fletcher School is an independent school with a program designed to build the academic, social, and emotional competence of learners with specific learning difficulties and/or ADHD (you can learn more about it at www.thefletcherschool.org). I first learned about Kaitlin's story when it was shared by my colleague Jenny Grabiec, who was their Director of Instructional Technology. At the beginning of second grade, Kaitlin was struggling with her writing, and this was having an impact on her motivation and overall outlook on learning. As her teachers commented, Kaitlin was "extremely creative" but she also had a "defeatist attitude" with "no incentive to try."

(continues)

(continued)

Journals were especially challenging to Kaitlin. She could not read what she had written just the day prior due to her poor spelling. Using the Dictation (Siri) feature on her iPad, Kaitlin started speaking her text into the Pages app before she would write in her journal. This process resulted in a significant improvement not only in Kaitlin's writing, but in her attitude and outlook. Kaitlin's third-grade teachers described her much differently, as someone who is "humorous, very creative, enjoys writing, friendly, and confident." As Kaitlin's experience demonstrates, sometimes a simple change can be all that's needed to have a positive impact on a learner's performance and attitude toward learning.

Photography

Mobile devices are almost always with us, at the ready for capturing those moments that would have been difficult to capture with a traditional camera. Although we often only consider the iPhone and other smartphones when we think about mobile photography, the iPad and similar tablets now have similarly powerful cameras, and many photography apps run on both types of devices.

Having learners take their own images for use in presentations and reports is a great way to start a conversation on copyright, digital citizenship, and other media literacy topics. When learners use their own images to create learning artifacts, they do not have to ask for permission, since they own the images they just created. We can then focus on other questions: what is the message or emotion I want to convey? How appropriate or relevant is the image to the rest of the content? Photography allows us to address critical thinking and communication skills.

One thing to keep in mind when using images and photography apps as part of classroom assignments is that not everyone may be able to see the images or use the apps. Aside from the built-in Camera app, most developers take for granted that people like me (with a significant visual impairment) would want to take photos. As a result, most photography apps are lacking when it comes to accessibility. For this reason, you should make sure there are always alternatives for photography activities to ensure all learners can participate.

 PAUSE AND THINK   As you think about some of the key historical events of the last hundred or so years, what are some of the iconic images that come to mind? How about in your personal history? What images stick out as reminders of important events, places, or people in your life?

In-class presentations are the most common way that learners are allowed to use images to demonstrate their understanding. Typically, learners will engage in some online research, and then present their findings and conclusions to the class in a slideshow that combines text and images. These kinds of presentations not only take away valuable classroom time, but they can also create a great deal of anxiety for learners who are not comfortable speaking in front of an audience (due to either language barriers or shyness).

SMART TIP The VoiceOver screen reader can use facial recognition to announce how many faces are in the frame and their relative locations. Using advanced object recognition, VoiceOver can also describe some of the objects in a photo.

One way to take some of the fear out of these presentations is to organize them as a gallery walk, where learners walk around the room and engage with each other in smaller groups. Several free or low-cost apps for iPad mirror the presentation capabilities of their desktop counterparts, including Apple's Keynote and Microsoft's PowerPoint.

To add some excitement to the typical presentation, we can give learners more freedom in how they present information by using alternative formats such as memes, collages, and even comics.

Memes

A meme is a captioned photo that is meant to be funny and shareable on social media. Memes usually rely on a character from a popular movie or some other cultural icon that is familiar to make an important point in a humorous way.

In the classroom, learners can use memes in several ways:

- Highlight the main idea or key concept (UDL: Highlight patterns, critical features, big ideas, and relationships). For example, they can highlight the main idea of a chapter in a novel, summarize a historical figure's importance, or illustrate the key relationships in a scientific or mathematical concept.

- Create posters for classroom rules and expectations that show the desired practices in a more memorable way.

- Provide prompts for strategies learners can employ for self-regulation in challenging situations (UDL: Facilitate personal coping skills and strategies).

Learners could use a number of online meme generators, but those services do not always filter out content that is intended for an adult audience. Apps that allow learners to combine text and images on the iPad, such as Adobe Spark Post, can provide a safer environment, especially if as a class you first create an album of images learners can use for their memes.

Collages

Collages are great for helping learners synthesize what they know about a given topic. A collage about the Incas could include a map of Peru, images of important landmarks such as Machu Picchu and the Inca Trail, and pictures of crops that were important to the Incas. Collages are a good match for any activity where it is important to have more than one image—for example, to show before-and-after, cause-and-effect, the order of historical events, and so on. Collages are also great for cultural activities that address traditions and help learners get to know each other better to build a sense of community (UDL: Foster collaboration and communication). Finally, collages can be used to document special experiences such as field trips or special assemblies, and share those experiences with parents to get them more involved in the life of the classroom and school.

Pic Collage is a great collage app for younger learners, whereas Diptic may be a better fit for older ones.

Comics

Comics do an excellent job of efficiently conveying a large amount of information in a short amount of space, because we can fill in the gaps between the individual cells. This makes them ideal for summarizing the content of an entire unit, work of literature, or project. Learners must make difficult choices as they decide what goes into the cells and their order, a process that actively engages them with the content. The Book Creator app, which will be discussed in more detail in the next chapter, includes a comic strip feature in its paid version. Other apps for creating comics include Strip Designer and Comic Life.

Photo Journals

Like the typical presentation assignment, photo journals combine images and text. Unlike a presentation, they are designed to stand alone from the presenter or speaker. For this reason, they require more explanation and thus more text. However, it is the interaction between the images and the text that results in the unique experience that can be provided with a photo journal. Although you could read the text to get a sense of what the story is about, it is the images that bring the content to life. A good example is a travel diary. Without the photos, the diary would not do as good a job of conveying the experience of the trip.

Any topic that could be presented in class could also be shared as a photo journal. Two of my favorite apps for creating photo journals on the iPad are Adobe Spark Page and Microsoft's Sway. Since photo journals will include more text, make sure you provide appropriate scaffolds and supports for writing to accommodate those learners who need them.

Audio

With apps such as GarageBand, learners who are gifted musically can create their own original compositions that can then be the soundtracks to podcasts and video projects. As with images taken with their own devices, students own the copyright to these original compositions and can use them as they choose. More important, they provide an outlet for the learners' creativity and give us another means of engaging the musicians and DJs in our classrooms with learning (UDL: Optimize relevance, value, and authenticity).

However, music is only one form of audio we can use in the classroom. With the microphones on mobile devices, audio also becomes a powerful data collection tool that can be used to document both learning and the history of the community. Audio still has advantages over video as a support for learning. Audio files tend to be smaller than video ones, which is an important consideration given the limited storage on the entry-level iPads many schools purchase to save money. The smaller file sizes also make audio files easier to share. Finally, audio can be more accessible to learners who have visual impairments (assuming their hearing is not also affected and the audio files are descriptive enough). Even then, a transcript should be provided for any audio-based media to ensure it doesn't create barriers for some learners.

Let's look at some activities that incorporate audio, beginning with some of the simplest ones and progressing to more complex ones such as podcasts.

Audio as a Scaffold for Writing

Even when writing is the goal of an activity, providing audio as a scaffold can be helpful. By starting with audio, we can reduce the anxiety that writing can cause for some learners. Once they have their most important thoughts down in audio form, we can proceed to the editing process with some momentum. Some of the editing can even be done while the content is in audio with some apps (we can split the audio and move the fragments around just as we would copy and paste text).

Audio Reflections

Reflection is one example of the kind of ongoing formative assessment that is an important component of a universally designed learning environment. It not only provides learners with an opportunity to summarize the key points of what they have just learned, but also provides valuable feedback for the teacher on how the lesson or unit is progressing. Based on this feedback, the teacher can then make any adjustments that are needed to ensure the needs of all learners are being met.

Reflection can take many forms, but a common one is a learning journal. Unfortunately, some learners grow anxious when asked to write down their thoughts, defeating the purpose of meaningful reflection. Because soliciting feedback and allowing them to reflect on learning, not the mechanics of writing, are the goals of the activity, using audio as an alternative is appropriate in this situation. With an app such as Just Press Record, the simple interface does not get in the way and it makes the app easy enough for even younger learners to use.

Once the reflection has been captured, it can be sent as an attachment to an email or text message. Even better, the audio file can be shared using the AirDrop device-to-device file-sharing feature of iOS.

SMART TIP   For even better sound, a simple sound booth can be a great maker project. All you need is a large cardboard box or a plastic tub and some sound-absorbing foam to line the inside of it (an "egg crate" mattress pad will also work in a pinch). To take the idea even further, you can use a camping tent to create a recording "nook" where learners can go to record their reflections with better privacy.

Oral History Projects

Oral history projects can engage learners by bringing history to life as they discover it from the perspective of those who were there to witness it (World War II veterans, Holocaust survivors, etc.). These kinds of projects don't have to be limited to history, however. Any topic that is of interest to learners is a potential oral history project. For example, learners can explore topics such as bullying that have an impact on their daily lives (UDL: Optimize relevance, value, and authenticity).

A great example is StoryCorps, which involves everyday people collecting stories that document the human experience in its various forms. The project has its own app, but learners can use any audio recording app to conduct this kind of oral history project while using StoryCorps as a model. Learners can go out into the community to get different perspectives on any given topic. In preparing for the interviews, they will also develop skills such as online research, planning, and time management.

Podcasts

A podcast (the word comes from combining iPod and broadcast) is an audio program that has new episodes automatically downloaded to a computer or mobile device on a regular schedule. One of my favorites is *This American Life* from National Public Radio (NPR). The stories featured on this podcast often combine audio recorded in the field, commentary, additional explanation from the in-studio hosts and reporters, and music meant to set an appropriate mood. This combination of interesting content and immersive production results in an engaging program that draws readers in, as evidenced by the fact that it is regularly near the top of most podcast lists as determined by number of downloads.

With an iPad and apps such as GarageBand, Opinion Podcasts, or Bossjock Studio, podcasting does not have to be limited to the radio producers at NPR. Any learner can create a podcast that includes original music and high-quality audio recordings from interviews with members of the community along with their own narration. For learners who are not musically inclined, GarageBand already includes loops that are ready for use in podcasts, or they can download royalty-free music from a number of sites (my favorite is Incompetech, at www.incompetech.com).

Video

Video is now the primary way many of us get our news and entertainment. Mobile devices have played a key role in the rise of video, as the tools we use both to consume the content and to create it. All it takes is pressing the record button on a smartphone or tablet and within minutes a video of what we just witnessed can be online for the entire world to see.

As educators, we can play a role in preparing our learners to be engaged citizens who can effectively use media to bring about change on the topics that matter most to them (student loan debt, budget cuts to education, and more) (UDL: Optimize relevance, value, and authenticity).

PAUSE AND THINK As you think about the news, what are some issues that have been brought to the public's attention thanks to the availability of video? How has the video shaped the perception of the issue? Whose perspective did the video represent? Whose was left out?

For many teens, video is a preferred means of communication. Rather than typing a message, they will often just record what is happening and share it with their peers with apps such as Instagram and Snapchat (or even live with apps such as Facebook Live). Often, we educators allow learners to communicate their understanding only in writing. This creates a disconnect between the ways our learners engage with the world in and out of school. Writing persuasively and skillfully is an important skill, and we should dedicate ample time to developing it. However, when appropriate to the goal of the lesson or unit, we can provide additional options that may be more engaging to today's media-savvy learners.

PAUSE AND THINK Have you ever asked your learners how they are using new tools and media for communication? After having a conversation on this topic with them, what are some ways you can incorporate what they have told you in your lesson plans?

When it comes to accessibility, video presents challenges for those who are not able to see or hear. As with photography, many video creation tools lack even the most basic accessibility support. From my own experience as a VoiceOver user, only the Apple apps, such as Clips and iMovie, have consistent support for accessibility. With other tools, developers don't seem to realize that people with a range of abilities want to use video as a tool for self-expression. One workaround is to have learners work in groups. A learner who is blind could still find a role in a group video project, drafting a script, researching online, or conducting interviews.

To make the content accessible to those who are deaf or hard of hearing, a transcript or captions need to be provided. In most cases, a transcript will be much easier to create, and with proper scaffolding it can provide an opportunity for learners to work on their writing as well. Starting with a transcript will also result in a smoother delivery when the video is recorded, and the transcript can be used as a starting point for captions. Some online services, such as YouTube, will accept a transcript and perform the timing to ensure the text is in sync with the video. This method of captioning tends to be much more accurate than the automatic captions YouTube provides, even though those can be edited as well. More recently, Apple introduced the Clips app, which uses voice recognition to turn the spoken audio into automatic captions (with an option for editing).

Video projects can be as simple as a quick reflection or as complex as group projects that require more planning and collaboration among several learners. The following are just a few examples of the ways you can use video to support learner-centered learning.

Video Reflections

Video has become easier to share and thus is a viable format for the kind of quick reflection mentioned in the section on audio. On the iPad, the built-in Camera app is ideal for this purpose. In addition to being already included with the device, the built-in app has great support for the accessibility features of iOS (including VoiceOver and Switch Control). The interface is also intuitive and easy to learn, offering just enough editing features (such as trimming to remove unwanted content at the beginning and end) that do not overwhelm the novice video editor.

For those who want more, the Clips app is the next step up. It provides title cards, fun filters (including a comic book one!), text and shape overlays to direct attention and highlight important points, and royalty-free music for a soundtrack. The finished product can be uploaded to video-sharing sites such as YouTube or Vimeo, or it can be shared directly with the teacher using the AirDrop file transfer feature.

Some learners may be shy about appearing on camera, and this could make them reluctant to use video as a form of reflection. It may also be that they just do not have a place at home they feel comfortable sharing with their peers. Fortunately, apps are available that allow learners to use a digital character and a virtual set to express their thoughts. One of my favorite apps for creating these kinds of avatars is ChatterPix. With ChatterPix, learners take a picture of an object and then draw a line over the part they want to speak. Once they record their audio, the object will appear to speak in sync with their recording. For younger learners, apps such as Sock Puppets, Puppet Pals HD, and Toontastic are available to allow them to record short videos as they move a character on a virtual stage.

Narrated Slideshows

As mentioned in the section on presentations, public speaking can be a source of anxiety for many learners. Another option for these learners is to allow them to record the presentation at home and upload it to a video-sharing site where it can be viewed by the entire class. This can be a good way to reduce the anxiety associated with whole-class presentations while still allowing learners to practice their public speaking skills (UDL: Minimize threats and distractions). Apps make it easy to create a presentation with audio narration. Two of my favorites are Adobe Spark Video and 30hands. Adobe Spark gives learners a head start by including a lot of free media for learners to use, such as royalty-free soundtracks and open source icons. Learners can work at their own pace by recording and re-recording the audio for each slide rather than for the entire presentation.

Green Screen Videos

Green screen (chroma keying) is a technique where a solid green or blue backdrop is removed in software and replaced with a different image or video. In the past, green screen was only possible on expensive sets with great lighting, but now any iPad with a green screen app (I use Green Screen by DoInk and TouchCast Studio) can perform this technique. All that's needed is an inexpensive green or blue backdrop that can be purchased at any crafts store.

With green screen, learners can be transported anywhere in the world: the surface of Mars, the halls of Congress, a rainforest, and more. Although green screen work has been a staple of media production classes, it can enhance learning in any subject. With a few props, learners can put themselves in a lab to explain scientific concepts, a courtroom to explain landmark court decisions, and much more.

 SMART TIP   If you want an object to appear to float in your green screen video, attach a cutout of the object to the end of a green straw like the ones available at Starbucks.

Stop-Motion Animation

As a kid, I remember purchasing a flip-book for learning how to throw a curveball from one of my favorite players at the time, Tom Seaver. As I flipped the pages of the book, I could see Mr. Seaver go through the entire pitching motion, one small step at a time. Stop-motion animation works in much the same way. Objects are placed against an appropriate backdrop and a photo is taken after each small change to create the illusion of movement when the entire sequence is played back as a video. Stop motion is perfect for documenting any process that takes place over time. The items used for the stop motion can range from paper cutouts to LEGOs to refrigerator magnets.

The recording itself can be done with an app such as iStopMotion.

Screencasts

A screencast is a special type of video where you record what you are doing on the screen as you explain a concept or idea. Any content that can be presented with visuals and voice narration is a good candidate for a screencast: from demonstrating how to use an app, to describing the parts of a cell, to showing the steps for solving a math problem or chemical equation. Apps such as Explain Everything provide everything you need to record a quality screencast, starting with a blank whiteboard where you can import your images and annotate them with a range of drawing tools while you provide your explanations with voice narration (UDL: Highlight patterns and critical features). Starting with iOS 11, a basic screen-recording feature is now available on the iPad. Screencasts are a great way to record videos you want your learners to review at home (the concept behind "flipping" the classroom). They are also a great way for learners to demonstrate their understanding and make their thinking visible as they explain key concepts and ideas to their peers.

Short Films

For some learners, video (and creative projects in general) can be a much-needed outlet for coping with difficult times in their lives. The iPad provides just about everything needed to create high-quality short films, especially when you combine a variety of tools from this chapter and previous ones: sketchnoting and note-taking apps to develop storyboards and scripts, photography apps for titles and other visuals, GarageBand for composing an original soundtrack, and finally powerful editing apps such as iMovie for pulling together a finished product learners can be excited about.

 SMART TIP   Use a tripod to capture better video by reducing the distracting camera shake that can take place when you hold your iPad. Since many tripods are designed to hold a traditional camera, you will also need to purchase a special mount. For versatility, try to purchase a universal mount that can be used with several iPad models.

Providing Formative Feedback

Before learners are ready to share their work with the rest of the world (which will be discussed in the next chapter), it's important that they receive sufficient feedback from their teachers and classmates to ensure it is their best work they are sharing. This kind of ongoing feedback, focused on continuous improvement for both learners and teachers, is known as formative assessment. Several services now exist that allow learners to quickly share content for formative assessment. Seesaw (http://web.seesaw.me/) and FreshGrade (www.freshgrade.com) are two such services that allow teachers to set up virtual classes where learners can document their understanding and growth over time using a variety of media and formats: video, photos, audio recordings, documents, or just a link to any resource they have posted on another website. With Seesaw, learners can also access a recordable whiteboard where they can create and share videos that combine text, drawing, and audio recording to explain their thinking (UDL: Vary the methods for response and navigation; Optimize individual choice and autonomy).

With either service, parents can log in on a separate iOS app to view and comment on their child's work. These apps also support notifications to ensure parents don't miss any updates when new work is posted, and they provide several ways to communicate with parents and involve them as active partners in the education of their children.

SKINNY SKETCH:
Christopher Hills

A lot of people view time spent on social media as an unproductive activity, but without social media I would never have met Christopher Hills. Christopher is a young man with cerebral palsy who lives on the other side of the world from me, in Queensland, Australia. I first learned about Christopher when a video he created, "One Head. One Switch. The World," went viral. In it, Christopher shared how he used a Mac with switch technology not only to edit the video itself, but also to attend an online school to pursue a certification in information technology.

Today he relies on the Switch Control accessibility feature to edit his videos with iMovie (iPad) and Final Cut (Mac). His skills as a video editor have given Christopher a strong voice as an advocate for the rights of people with disabilities, especially when it comes to technology and innovation access. As he stated in an interview with the Huffington Post:

With Switch Control, I am still limited. But it's no longer my body that limits me; it is only my imagination. There has never been a more exciting time to have a disability. Technology is at the heart of the modern world.

(continues)

(continued)

It has never been easier to make a valuable contribution to society, regardless of your abilities.

Christopher and I are now collaborators. We co-wrote an interactive book focusing on Switch Control that leverages both of our talents. Writing is easier for me due to the time it takes to type for a switch user, but Christopher's talents as a video editor and storyteller far surpass mine. It has been a beautiful collaboration that would not have been possible were it not for social media.

Christopher Hills PHOTO: GARRY HILLS

 A CLOSER LOOK Scan the QR code to access additional resources for this chapter, including a student activity, on the companion website.

Key Takeaways

□ The iPad includes supports that can be used to scaffold writing when that is the goal of the lesson.

□ The iPad is a versatile tool for content creation with a variety of media including photos, audio, video, and animation.

□ For many of our learners, portable audio and video media (especially tablets and phones) dominate their communication, enabling them to take their activities outside the classroom and into more authentic, real-world contexts.

□ No single medium is perfectly accessible to all learners. As we incorporate multimedia learning into our lessons, we need to consider the barriers different media and content creation tools could present to some learners who need accessibility support, and we should be ready to provide alternatives to ensure these learners can participate in the same activities as their peers.

5

Publishing and Sharing Beyond the Classroom

*I*t's race day and as you pull up to the starting line you reflect on how far you've come. At one point, you needed lots of help just to stay on the bike, but now you are an expert rider. Your form reflects years of practice, and you are also well versed in the strategies needed to succeed. You know when to go hard, and when to draft and conserve your energy. With every race, you have learned more about both your body and your equipment (including your bike). Loose and relaxed, you trust that you are ready to excel. "You've got this," you tell yourself.

When using technology to enhance learning, we all start out as novices that require varying levels of support. Over time we become more skilled and confident through practice. As with riding a bike, we may at some point out-grow the challenge that we get from riding with the same people and in the same places all the time.

To keep growing and developing our expertise, we need to take it to the next level. As riders, we may seek out more skilled riders who will challenge and inspire us. We can sign up for a race, where we will be competing not only against other riders but also against our own previous times. Using what we learn from each race and from other riders, we can continue to improve.

Learners can do the same thing by publishing to a broader audience. By publishing a blog post or video online, we are sending an important message: our work is valuable and worth sharing. This can by itself have a powerful impact on motivation and engagement. Time and time again I have witnessed how learners raise the bar when they know the work is going to be shared beyond the four walls of the classroom. It is just human nature to put our best foot forward when we know we are going to be in the spotlight. When implemented as part of project-based learning, publishing to a wider audience can also make learning more authentic by helping learners make connections between what they have learned in the classroom and the real world as represented by the comments and other feedback from those who view their work once it is published. These exchanges can also give our learners practice with the kinds of interactions they will likely engage in as they enter a world of work that is increasingly moving online.

This chapter will focus on tools learners can use to publish content beyond the classroom. These tools are intended to bring it all together by allowing learners to collect the various photos, videos, audio recordings, and other artifacts they have created into one cohesive work that can be more easily shared online. With these tools, learners can build digital portfolios that show a selection of their best work (and hopefully increase their access to better college and career opportunities). They can also use these digital portfolios to start building a positive digital footprint and a strong personal brand that presents them in the best light possible. In the process, we can explore important digital citizenship skills our learners need to gain if they are to be effective communicators in online communities where they will be exposed to people of diverse backgrounds and perspectives.

At this level of technology expertise, learners are not just using media to demonstrate their understanding of academic concepts in the classroom; they are using it to look beyond the classroom and become agents for change in their communities as they develop a unique voice and express their positions on the important issues that impact their lives. You have already seen a great example of this process in action with the Skinny Sketch at the end of the previous chapter. Video provided a way for Christopher Hills to demonstrate his understanding in a way that writing (which takes considerable effort for him to do) could not. However, as Christopher developed his skills as a video editor, videos shared on his YouTube channel became the primary way he advocates for better inclusion for people like himself. Through his videos, Christopher has connected with organizations that have a similar vision, exponentially increasing his reach and the impact of his work. I would like to see the same for all learners.

If the first part of this book is about the "where" (making the learning environment more accessible) and the "what" of learning (removing the barriers that arise from the use of print as the dominant media), then this final chapter is all about the "who." The goal is to encourage learners to share their creative works more broadly so that they begin to see themselves not only as learners, but as active participants in the political, social, and cultural life of their information-driven society.

Blogs and Websites

Once learners are ready to share their work more publicly, they can graduate to a public blog or website. Not long ago, creating a new blog or website required an understanding of HTML, the language that tells a web browser how to display web pages. Today, much of this process has been simplified by the emergence of content management systems (CMSs). With a CMS, the person creating the blog or website simply enters the text into a visual editor not too different from the word processing software many of us already use on our computers. Adding images and other media is similarly simple. There are many options for quickly publishing a new blog or website; my favorite is WordPress.

With just a few clicks, learners can set up a free website at Wordpress.com and select from several eye-catching designs that have been designed to work well on both desktop and mobile web browsers. A few of these designs have been designated as "accessibility-ready," meaning that they have undergone testing to ensure accessibility for users of assistive technologies. With these WordPress themes, we can start a conversation about accessibility with our learners: why it is needed, and how they can get started with a few simple techniques that will make their sites or blogs more accessible. One example is the addition of alternative text to images. Screen readers, including VoiceOver on iOS devices, can use the alternative text to describe the images to someone who is blind.

The initial setup for a WordPress blog or website is probably best done from a computer, but ongoing posts can be performed from a mobile device with the free WordPress app. The key difference between a blog and a website is that websites can include pages to group related content into different sections accessed through a menu at the top of the page. With a blog, content appears on one page in the order it was submitted. The idea is that the pages of a website are more static, whereas a blog contains frequently updated content.

With WordPress, learners can have the best of both worlds. They can create a website with sections for a personal introduction, a résumé, a photo gallery showing projects they have completed, awards they have won, and more. Within this site, a blog can include ongoing reflections related to work in progress, responses to questions raised in class, and so on. A carefully curated website can be a good way for learners to start building a personal brand that makes them stand out from the crowd when applying for college or looking for an internship or job.

 SMART TIP Ideally, learners will use their own images to add visual appeal to their blog posts, but this is not always possible. Public domain or Creative Commons images can be used without violating copyright laws. Two of my favorite sites for these images are Unsplash and Pixabay. Most of the time, all that is required for using a photo is an attribution or citation, which is a good digital citizenship habit for learners to pick up anyway.

TouchCast

I already mentioned TouchCast in the previous chapter as a powerful video editing solution that supports the creation of green screen videos, but TouchCast can also be used to provide learners with another option for showcasing their digital portfolios. A TouchCast is an interactive, "touchable" video that combines the expressiveness of video with the interactivity of the web. Each TouchCast video can include interactive overlays (video apps, or "vApps") that viewers can tap or click to access additional content in a variety of formats: web pages, photos, other videos, documents, and more. Clicking on an overlay or vApp will pause the video to allow sufficient time to review the linked content, resuming playback when the vApp is closed. The media introduction for this chapter was created with TouchCast.

TouchCast can host the finished videos on its servers, but there is also an option to share a noninteractive version on YouTube. This YouTube version can be helpful for providing a captioned version of the video, since TouchCast does not support captioning as of this writing.

Book Creator

With the Book Creator app, any learner can be a published author whose book is available to a worldwide audience. By design, the app provides learners with a blank canvas where they can add content with any of the media creation tools available on the iPad. Each page can include text boxes, photos, and videos taken with the iPad's camera, audio recordings, and drawings. Helpful aids such as guidelines and snapping ensure items are aligned correctly, and just about every aspect of the page, from the color of the background to the size of the text and font, is customizable. The simplicity of Book Creator makes it possible for even younger learners to publish their own books. The free version of the app includes all the functionality of the paid version, but it is limited to one book. The paid version also includes comic book layouts with speech bubbles and stickers.

Once a book is ready to publish, this can be done in a variety of ways depending on the desired level of privacy. Book Creator can output an industry-standard ePub version of the book that can be published on Apple's iBooks Store. For learners who do not own a mobile device to read ePub books, an option to publish a video of the book to YouTube or Vimeo is also available. That version of the book will include page-flip animations, and it will play any embedded media sequentially within the video. More recently, Book Creator added the ability to publish books online at bookcreator.com. However, for privacy reasons, these books can only be published by a teacher with an educator account. Once it's published, the teacher can share a link to the book, which can also be read online with a web reader.

From an accessibility perspective, Book Creator includes features for providing an optimal reading experience for all learners. The app includes a built-in Read to Me feature to support decoding. Learners could use the built-in text to speech features of iOS to do the same thing, but with Book Creator's version there is no need to select or perform a special gesture, two actions that could be difficult for younger learners or those with motor difficulties. All learners must do to use the Read to Me feature is tap a few times to start listening to the book as it is read aloud with word highlighting. An option for automatic page flips can also be turned on for readers who have motor difficulties that make the page flip gesture difficult.

To ensure content created with the app is accessible, the Book Creator app has an option for adding an accessibility description for any image or video added to a book. This ensures the images and videos added to a book have text alternatives that can be used by a screen reader to describe this content to someone who is blind. Of course, teachers should make learners aware of this feature and encourage them to add descriptions to all their books.

Book Creator has a web version that works on Chromebooks and other devices that can run the Chrome web browser.

 A CLOSER LOOK   Scan the QR code to access additional resources for this chapter, including student activities, on the book's companion website.

Key Takeaways

◻ When we encourage learners to share their work with a broader audience, we send a powerful message: their work is valuable and worth sharing. This can by itself help raise the bar on the quality of the work they create.

◻ Sharing beyond the classroom is also an important step toward preparing our learners to be digital citizens who can interact with people from a variety of backgrounds and perspectives in the online spaces that will dominate the world of work in the future.

◻ With the tools mentioned in this chapter, learners can create dynamic digital portfolios that allow them to share their best work with the rest of the world. A digital portfolio brings together the various digital artifacts learners create (their writing, photos, videos, and audio recordings) into one cohesive work that can be more easily shared online. These digital portfolios can take the form of a blog or website (WordPress), an interactive video (TouchCast), or an e-book (Book Creator).

Conclusion

Congratulations! You have made it through your first reading of this book. Instead of stopping here, I encourage you to go back through each chapter and explore the apps and other resources with your own learners. If you are reluctant to implement technology because it seems overwhelming, remember that you don't have to master its use all at once. You can start small by picking just one app or activity to try out with your learners in one lesson or unit. Over time, the process will become more familiar and you will gain confidence and skill. Just like an expert rider, you will get better with practice. As you do, you will be modeling important elements of expert learning in your classroom: taking chances, reflecting on the experience, and taking a different approach based on what you have learned.

Although the goal of this book is to move all learners to a more transformative use of mobile technology, remember that all learners vary and will advance at their own pace. However, even the small steps can make a big difference. For a learner who is currently struggling to read due to vision challenges or dyslexia, just discovering the text-to-speech features on the iPad could be the difference between shutting down and turning off from learning and receiving the encouragement needed to continue.

I would love to hear from you and see the wonderful things you are able to do with the tools discussed in this book. By sharing your work, you will be contributing to a richer experience for future readers who may get additional inspiration. To share your work with me (once you have received the appropriate permissions), upload it to any online service where I can access it, and then send a link to lfperez@me.com. I look forward to seeing the creative ways in which you use mobile devices to empower your learners with their own "adjustable seats for learning."

References

Gemsbacher, M. (2015). Video captions benefit everyone. *Policy Insights in Behavioral and Brain Science, 2*(1), 195–202.

Lave, J., & Wenger, E. (1990). Situated learning: Legitimate peripheral participation. Cambridge, UK: Cambridge University Press.

Meyer, A., & Rose, D. H. (2005). The future is in the margins: The role of technology and disability in educational reform. In D. H. Rose, A. Meyer & C. Hitchcock (Eds.), *The universally designed classroom: Accessible curriculum and digital technologies* (pp. 13–35). Cambridge, MA: Harvard Education Press.

Meyer, A., Rose, D. H., & Gordon, D. (2014) *Universal design for learning: Theory and practice.* Wakefield, MA: CAST Professional Publishing.

Traxler, J. (2007). Defining, discussing and evaluating mobile learning: The moving finger writes and having writ... [sic], *International Review of Research in Open and Distributed Learning, 8*(2). Retrieved from www.irrodl.org/index.php/irrodl/article/view/346/875.

Appendix

Top 10 Apps Mentioned in the Book

This table lists the top 10 apps mentioned in the book, in the order in which they appear. These are my go-to apps that I use the most, and the ones that I have found to offer the most flexibility in terms of what I can do with them.

Note that apps sometimes go on sale. The prices listed are accurate as of the time the table was compiled.

App Name	Category	Price	Why it made the list
Voice Dream Reader	Text to Speech	$14.99	A highly customizable text-to-speech app, with support for commercial voices, dyslexia-friendly fonts, and much more.
MindNode	Concept Mapping	$9.99	The only concept mapping app I have found with VoiceOver support.

App Name	Category	Price	Why it made the list
Google Keep	Reminders Notes	Free	A cross-platform solution with many ways to capture information: text, photos, and audio. Can search text inside photos with OCR.
Notability	Notes	$9.99	Records audio that can be synced to text and annotations. Great for lectures and longer presentations.
Adobe Spark Video	Narrated Presentations	Free	Makes it possible to create a narrated presentation in minutes with professional-quality templates and access to an extensive collection of Creative Commons images, icons, and soundtracks.
Clips	Video	Free	Uses speech recognition to automatically create captions for the short videos you create and share on social media.
iMovie	Video	Free	An easy-to-learn yet powerful video-editing app with just about everything you need to create a video, including professional-level titles, soundtracks, and a built-in voice narration tool. Has a trailers feature for creating fun movie trailers with motion graphics and Hollywood-style effects.
Explain Everything	Video	$9.99	Records the screen as you use voice narration and annotation to explain difficult concepts visually.

App Name	Category	Price	Why it made the list
TouchCast	Video	Free	Creates interactive videos with embedded vApps (video apps), support for green screen, whiteboard features for video annotation, and more.
Book Creator	eBook Authoring	$4.99	Creates industry-standard ePub books with rich media content (images, audio, video, and drawings). Has comic book layouts.

Introducing the
CAST Skinny Books™

"Don't tell me everything. Just give me the skinny!"

Skinny Books by CAST address critical topics of education practice through brief, informative publications that emphasize practical tips and strategies. We talk about these books as "multivitamins"—densely packed with helpful knowledge in a small, digestible format.

Learning on the Go by Luis F. Pérez is the first in the Skinny Books series. Future titles will address topics such as math education, arts in education, formative assessment, teaching ELLs, tips for improving the college classroom, and much more.

We welcome new proposals. Got an idea? Let us know at *publishing@cast.org*.

While every Skinny Book will be in tune with the inclusive principles of Universal Design for Learning, not every title needs to address UDL specifically. For those that do, the authors may assume readers have a knowledge of UDL already, as we've done in *Learning on the Go.*

If you need an introduction to UDL, check out our free online multimedia book *Universal Design for Learning: Theory & Practice* published at *http://udltheorypractice .cast.org.*

You can also purchase this or many other titles on UDL from *www.castpublishing.org*.